Love in Verse

Love in Verse

CLASSIC POEMS

of

THE HEART

COLLECTED BY

KATHLEEN BLEASE

FAWCETT BOOKS

The Random House Publishing Group • New York

A Fawcett Book
Published by The Random House Publishing Group

Introduction and compilation copyright © 1998 The Random House
Publishing Group, a division of Random House, Inc.

Published in the United States by Fawcett Books, an imprint of
The Random House Publishing Group, a division of
Random House, Inc., New York, and simultaneously in Canada
by Random House of Canada Limited, Toronto.

Fawcett is a registered trademark and the Fawcett colophon is a
trademark of Random House, Inc.

www.ballantinebooks.com

Library of Congress Cataloging-in-Publication Data
Love in verse / collected by Kathleen Blease.
p.   cm.
ISBN 0-449-00128-8 (pbk.)
1. Love poetry, English.   2. Love poetry, American.
I. Blease, Kathleen.
PR1184.L46   1998
811.008′03543—dc21   97-29400
                                              CIP

Cover design by Heather Kern

Book design by Ruth Kolbert

Manufactured in the United States of America

First Edition: February 1998

13 15 17 19 20 18 16 14 12

TO MY LOVE,

Roger

CONTENTS

❊

ACKNOWLEDGMENTS   xii

INTRODUCTION   xiii

I
Love Finally Found

Love's Philosophy   *Percy Bysshe Shelley*   3

The Years   *Sara Teasdale*   4

The Song of Songs (from Chapter 2)   *The Bible*   5

Sonnet   *(Major Robert) Calder Campbell*   6

The Dream   *Aphra Behn*   7

To Citriodora   *Philip Henry Savage*   8

To ——   *John Brainard*   9

A White Rose   *John Boyle O'Reilly*   10

Thomas Ford's Music of Sundry Kinds (excerpt)

    Thomas Ford   11

A Dream Within a Dream   *Edgar Allan Poe*   13

The Open Window   *Edward Rowland Sill*   14

A Sonnet of the Moon   *Charles Best*   16

A Valentine   *Mathilda Betham-Edwards*   17

I Hid My Love   *John Clare*   18

The Lips That Love's Own Hand Did Make
  William Shakespeare 19

The Thought of Her   *Richard Hovey* 20

Love's Springtide   *Frank Dempster Sherman* 21

Summer   *John Clare* 22

The Look   *Sara Teasdale* 23

Valentines (written for Miss L——'s Valentine
  Parties)   *Grace Greenwood* 24

The Fair Singer   *Andrew Marvell* 25

Sudden Light   *Dante Gabriel Rossetti* 26

Air and Angels   *John Donne* 27

The Definition of Love   *Andrew Marvell* 29

Absent Yet Present   *Edward Bulwer-Lytton* 31

Love   *George Herbert* 33

A Birthday   *Christina Rossetti* 34

Jenny Kissed Me   *Leigh Hunt* 35

A Song: When June Is Past, the Fading Rose
  Thomas Carew 36

I Lived with Visions   *Elizabeth Barrett Browning* 37

The String Around My Finger   *John Brainard* 38

On a Girdle   *Edmund Waller* 40

Give All to Love   *Ralph Waldo Emerson* 41

Love Me Not for Comely Grace   *John Wilbye* 43

Meeting at Night   *Robert Browning* 44

Song to Amarantha, That She Would
  Dishevel Her Hair   *Richard Lovelace* 45

She Walks in Beauty   *Lord Byron* 47

My Star   *Robert Browning* 48

Desire   *Samuel Taylor Coleridge* 49

The Love I Bear Thee   *Elizabeth Barrett Browning* 50

Sunday up the River (excerpt)   *James Thomson*   51

The Kiss   *Sara Teasdale*   52

On a Fair Morning, As I Came by the Way
    Thomas Morley   53

The Wine of Love   *James Thomson*   54

II

Dreams of the Future

To Celia   *Sir Charles Sedley*   57

Wedding Prayer   *Traditional Apache Prayer*   58

I Will Make You Brooches
    Robert Louis Stevenson   59

To Celia   *Ben Jonson*   60

Beauty That Is Never Old
    James Weldon Johnson   61

Song   *Edgar Allan Poe*   62

Come, My Celia   *Ben Jonson*   63

Most Sweet It Is   *William Wordsworth*   64

Shall I Compare Thee   *William Shakespeare*   65

Love Thyself Last   *Ella Wheeler Wilcox*   66

To Anthea, Who May Command Him Anything
    Robert Herrick   67

Don't Tell the World That You're Waiting for Me
    Eliza Cook   69

My Dear and Only Love
    James Graham, Marquis of Montrose   70

A Praise of His Love
    Henry Howard, Earl of Surrey   72

The Passionate Shepherd to His Love
    Christopher Marlowe   74

The Nymph's Reply to the Shepherd
    Sir Walter Raleigh   76

If Thou Must Love Me
    Elizabeth Barrett Browning   78

Love Is Enough: Song I   *William Morris*   79

To Jane   *Percy Bysshe Shelley*   80

After Parting   *Sara Teasdale*   82

When, Dearest, I But Think on Thee
    Owen Felltham   83

How Do I Love Thee?
    Elizabeth Barrett Browning   85

III
A Life Together

Music, When Soft Voices Die
    Percy Bysshe Shelley   89

Love's Calendar   *Thomas Bailey Aldrich*   90

Art (excerpt)   *James Thomson*   91

Love Is Love   *Sir Edward Dyer*   92

The Marriage of True Minds
    William Shakespeare   93

Love's Emblems   *Grace Greenwood*   94

Song   *Thomas Lovell Beddoes*   95

To F——   *Edgar Allan Poe*   96

Delia (34)   *Samuel Daniel*   97

She Was a Phantom of Delight
    William Wordsworth   98

Life and Love   *Elizabeth Barrett Browning*   100

My Mistress' Eyes   *William Shakespeare*   101

One Day I Wrote Her Name   *Edmund Spenser*   102

"And Forgive Us Our Trespasses"   *Aphra Behn*   *103*

In the Valley of Cauteretz   *Alfred Lord Tennyson*   *104*

Believe Me, If All Those Endearing Young Charms
    Thomas Moore   *105*

The First Day   *Christina Rossetti*   *106*

The Love Is Better Than High Birth to Me
    William Shakespeare   *107*

Song   *Richard Le Gallienne*   *108*

If Ever I Have Thought or Said
    Philip Henry Savage   *109*

My Beautiful Lady   *Thomas Woolner*   *110*

To Me, Fair Friend, You Never Can Be Old
    William Shakespeare   *112*

The Presence of Love   *Samuel Taylor Coleridge*   *113*

Most Happy Letters   *Edmund Spenser*   *114*

Serénade   *Edgar Allan Poe*   *115*

Love in a Life   *Robert Browning*   *116*

My Love in Her Attire   *Anonymous*   *117*

The Indian Serenade   *Percy Bysshe Shelley*   *118*

To Asra   *Samuel Taylor Coleridge*   *119*

The Revelation   *Coventry Patmore*   *120*

Oh! That We Two Were Maying
    Charles Kingsley   *121*

A Red, Red Rose   *Robert Burns*   *122*

To My Dear and Loving Husband
    Anne Bradstreet   *123*

INDEX OF AUTHORS   *124*

INDEX OF FIRST LINES   *127*

ACKNOWLEDGMENTS

Writers over the generations, the masters and those less celebrated alike, are truly responsible for this book. Nevertheless, the undertaking of putting together this collection required the cooperation and consideration of others. My gratitude goes to my friend, colleague, and editor Elizabeth Zack for proposing the idea, then giving me the freedom to develop it. Along the way my loved ones sat and watched while I researched and organized, going without home-cooked meals and other amenities, and so I thank my family, Roger and Ben, for their understanding. I can't pass this moment, of course, without showing my appreciation to the writers whose verses have endured the test of time. Once again, they are watching us enjoy their wisdom, and I'd like to thank them personally for their immortal inspiration.

INTRODUCTION

WHEN LOVE IS FINALLY FOUND it dramatically alters daily routine; the mundane becomes exciting and refreshing. The body breathes again, taking deep breaths as it once did as a child, and everything has an unmistakable aroma. The water, air, and trees just outside the window fill the head with scent, and at last, the face in the mirror looks like the person it always wanted to be; it's gleaming, rosy, and smiling. And it doesn't matter who notices, and if it did, a mask would be fruitless. True love simply cannot be hidden. It radiates the undeniable quality of *feeling alive*!

The path we travel before love is found often seems to be a tangent without destination, but then love steps in front of us and our destination is made perfectly clear. The path brought us right here. Arriving at a beautiful surprise, arriving at love. The first time two hearts connect, that is the day to mark and celebrate, for it's the birthday of life. The first day of life as it should be! A rebirth and a new vision. It's now obvious how each day is meant to be spent.

Love is one of the last natural elements that is truly free. Yet it brings an abundance of joy and success and makes even the least of material things seem plentiful. It's magical, revitalizing, eye-opening, and most of all, never-ending.

It's human nature to want to fall in love. The deep desire to connect with another's soul, to understand someone's thoughts without the spoken word, to communicate clearly with touch: this is the common thread that weaves together the generations, the genders, and all the creeds and cultures.

And so it is little wonder that over the years writers dedicated their vision and pens to the task of defining love on paper, capturing the power enveloped in the emotion, way of life, and endless passion love cultivates. Many became dedicated to the subject and found it an endless source of inspiration, and their creations live with us still. Their words are as clear and as significant as on the day they were written.

Love in Verse celebrates the joys of finding true love. These poems, like fine art, share qualities that will touch us for a lifetime. Enjoy them with the one who's captured your heart.

I

Love
Finally
Found

LOVE'S PHILOSOPHY

The fountains mingle with the river,
 And the rivers with the ocean;
The winds of heaven mix forever,
 With a sweet emotion;
Nothing in the world is single;
 All things by a law divine
In one another's being mingle:—
 Why not I with thine?

See! the mountains kiss high heaven,
 And the waves clasp one another;
No sister flower would be forgiven
 If it disdained its brother;
And the sunlight clasps the earth,
 And the moonbeams kiss the sea:—
What are all these kissings worth,
 If thou kiss not me?

PERCY BYSSHE SHELLEY
[1792–1822]

THE YEARS

To-night I close my eyes and see
A strange procession passing me—
The years before I saw your face
Go by me with a wistful grace;
They pass, the sensitive shy years,
As one who strives to dance, half blind with tears.

The years went by and never knew
That each one brought me nearer you;
Their path was narrow and apart
And yet it led me to your heart—
Oh sensitive shy years, oh lonely years,
That strove to sing with voices drowned in tears.

SARA TEASDALE
[1884–1933]

THE SONG OF SONGS
(from Chapter 2)

The voice of my beloved!
Behold, he cometh leaping upon the mountains,
Skipping upon the hills.
My beloved is like a roe or a young hart.
Behold, he standeth behind our wall,
He looketh forth at the windows,
Showing himself through the lattice.
My beloved spake, and said unto me,
"Rise up, my love, my fair one, and come away.
For, lo, the winter is past,
The rain is over and gone;
The flowers appear on the earth;
The time of the singing of birds is come,
And the voice of the turtle is heard in our land;
The fig tree putteth forth her green figs,
And the vines with the tender grape give a good smell.
Arise, my love, my fair one, and come away.

"O my dove, that art in the clefts of the rock,
In the secret places of the stairs,
Let me see thy countenance,
Let me hear thy voice;
For sweet is thy voice,
And thy countenance is comely."

THE BIBLE

SONNET

When midst the summer-roses the warm bees
   Are swarming in the sun, and thou—so full
   Of innocent glee—dost with thy white hands pull
Pink scented apples from the garden trees
To fling at me, I catch them, on my knees,
   Like those who gather'd manna; and I cull
   Some hasty buds to pelt thee—white as wool
Lilies, or yellow jonquils, or heartsease;—
Then I can speak my love, ev'n tho' thy smiles
   Gush out among thy blushes, like a flock
Of bright birds from rose-bowers; but when thou'rt gone
   I have no speech,—no magic that beguiles,
   The stream of utterance from the harden'd rock:—
The dial cannot speak without the sun!

(MAJOR ROBERT) CALDER CAMPBELL
[1798–1857]

6

THE DREAM

All trembling in my arms Aminta lay,
Defending of the bliss I strove to take;
Raising my rapture by her kind delay,
Her force so charming was and weak.
The soft resistance did betray the grant,
While I pressed on the heaven of my desires;
Her rising breasts with nimbler motions pant;
Her dying eyes assume new fires.
Now to the height of languishment she grows,
And still her looks new charms put on;
Now the last mystery of Love she knows,
We sigh, and kiss: I waked, and all was done.

'Twas but a dream, yet by my heart I knew,
Which still was panting, part of it was true:
Oh how I strove the rest to have believed;
Ashamed and angry to be undeceived!

APHRA BEHN
[1640–1689]

TO CITRIODORA

I turn and see you passing in the street
When you are not. I take another way,
Lest missing you the fragrance of the day
Exhale, and I know not that it is sweet.
And marking you I follow, and when we meet
Love laughs to see how sudden I am gay;
Sweetens the air with fragrance like a spray
Of sweet verbena, and bids my heart to beat.

Love laughs; and girls that take you by the hand,
Know that a sweet thing has befallen them;
And women give their hearts into your heart.
There is, I think, no man in all the land
But would be glad to touch your garment's hem.
And I, I love you with a love apart.

PHILIP HENRY SAVAGE
[1868–1899]

TO ——

❀

—She was a lovely one—her shape was light
And delicately flexible; her eye
Might have been black, or blue,—but it was bright,
Though beaming not on every passer-by;
'T was very modest, and a little shy.
The eyelash seemed to shade the very cheek;
That had the color of a sunset sky,
Not rosy—but a soft and heavenly streak
For which the arm might strike—the heart might
        break—
And a soft gentle voice, that kindly sweet
Accosted one she chanced to overtake,
While walking slowly on iambic feet,
In tones that fell as soft as heaven's own dew—
Who was it! dear young Lady, was it you?

JOHN BRAINARD
[1796–1828]

————

9

A WHITE ROSE

The red rose whispers of passion,
   And the white rose breathes of love;
Oh, the red rose is a falcon,
   And the white rose is a dove.

But I send you a cream-white rosebud,
   With a flush on its petal tips;
For the love that is purest and sweetest
   Has a kiss of desire on the lips.

JOHN BOYLE O'REILLY
[1844–1890]

THOMAS FORD'S MUSIC
OF SUNDRY KINDS *(excerpt)*

There is a lady sweet and kind,
Was never face so pleas'd my mind;
I did but see her passing by,
And yet I love her till I die.

Her gesture, motion, and her smiles,
Her wit, her voice, my heart beguiles,
Beguiles my heart, I know not why,
And yet I love her till I die.

Her free behaviour, winning looks,
Will make a lawyer burn his books;
I touch'd her not, alas! not I,
And yet I love her till I die.

Had I her fast betwixt mine arms,
Judge you that think such sports were harms,
Were't any harm? no, no, fie, fie,
For I will love her till I die.

Should I remain confined there
So long as Phoebus in his sphere,
I to request, she to deny,
Yet would I love her till I die.

Cupid is winged and doth range,
Her country so my love doth change:
But change she earth, or change she sky,
Yet will I love her till I die.

THOMAS FORD
[1580?–1648]

A DREAM WITHIN A DREAM

*T*ake this kiss upon the brow!
And, in parting from you now,
Thus much let me avow—
You are not wrong, who deem
That my days have been a dream:
Yet if hope has flown away
In a night, or in a day,
In a vision, or in none,
Is it therefore the less *gone*?
All that we see or seem
Is but a dream within a dream.

I stand amid the roar
Of a surf-tormented shore,
And I hold within my hand
Grains of the golden sand—
How few! yet how they creep
Through my fingers to the deep,
While I weep—while I weep!
O God! can I not grasp
Them with a tighter clasp?
O God! can I not save
One from the pitiless wave?
Is *all* that we see or seem
But a dream within a dream?

EDGAR ALLAN POE
[1809–1849]

THE OPEN WINDOW

My tower was grimly builded,
   With many a bolt and bar,
"And here," I thought, "I will keep my life
   From the bitter world afar."

Dark and chill was the stony floor,
   Where never a sunbeam lay,
And the mould crept up on the dreary wall,
   With its ghost touch, day by day.

One morn, in my sullen musings,
   A flutter and cry I heard;
And close at the rusty casement
   There clung a frightened bird.

Then back I flung the shutter
   That was never before undone,
And I kept till its wings were rested
   The little weary one.

But in through the open window,
   Which I had forgot to close,
There had burst a gush of sunshine
   And a summer scent of rose.

For all the while I had burrowed
   There in my dingy tower,
Lo! the birds had sung and the leaves had danced
   From hour to sunny hour.

And such balm and warmth and beauty
   Came drifting in since then,
That window still stands open
   And shall never be shut again.

EDWARD ROWLAND SILL
[1841–1887]

———

A SONNET OF THE MOON

*L*ook how the pale queen of the silent night
Doth cause the ocean to attend upon her,
And he, as long as she is in his sight,
With her full tide is ready her to honor.
But when the silver waggon of the moon
Is mounted up so high he cannot follow,
The sea calls home his crystal waves to moan,
And with low ebb doth manifest his sorrow.
So you that are the sovereign of my heart
Have all my joys attending on your will;
My joys low-ebbing when you do depart,
When you return their tide my heart doth fill.
So as you come and as you do depart,
Joys ebb and flow within my tender heart.

CHARLES BEST
[*early 17th century*]

A VALENTINE

*W*hat shall I send my sweet today,
   When all the woods attune in love?
   And I would show the lark and dove,
That I can love as well as they.

I'll send a locket full of hair,—
   But no, for it might chance to lie
   Too near her heart, and I should die
Of love's sweet envy to be there.

A violet is sweet to give,—
   Ah, stay! she'd touch it with her lips,
   And, after such complete eclipse,
How could my soul consent to live?

I'll send a kiss, for that would be
   The quickest sent, the lightest borne,
   And well I know tomorrow morn
She'll send it back again to me.

Go, happy winds; ah, do not stay,
   Enamoured of my lady's cheek,
   But hasten home, and I'll bespeak
Your services another day!

MATHILDA BETHAM-EDWARDS
[1776–1852]

I HID MY LOVE

I hid my love when young till I
Couldn't bear the buzzing of a fly;
I hid my love to my despite
Till I could not bear to look at light:
I dare not gaze upon her face
But left her memory in each place;
Where'er I saw a wild flower lie
I kissed and bade my love good-bye.

I met her in the greenest dells,
Where dewdrops pearl the wood bluebells;
The lost breeze kissed her bright blue eye,
The bee kissed and went singing by,
A sunbeam found a passage there,
A gold chain round her neck so fair;
As secret as the wild bee's song
She lay there all the summer long.

I hid my love in field and town
Till e'en the breeze would knock me down;
The bees seemed singing ballads o'er,
The fly's bass turned a lion's roar;
And even silence found a tongue,
To haunt me all the summer long;
The riddle nature could not prove
Was nothing else but secret love.

JOHN CLARE
[1793–1864]

THOSE LIPS THAT LOVE'S OWN HAND
DID MAKE

Those lips that Love's own hand did make
Breath'd forth the sound that said "I hate"
To me that languish'd for her sake;
But when she saw my woeful state,
Straight in her heart did mercy come,
Chiding that tongue that, ever sweet,
Was us'd in giving gentle doom,
And taught it thus anew to greet:
"I hate" she alter'd with an end
That follow'd it as gentle day
Doth follow night, who like a fiend
From heaven to hell is flown away:
    "I hate" from hate away she threw,
    And sav'd my life, saying "not you."

WILLIAM SHAKESPEARE
[1564–1616]

———

THE THOUGHT OF HER

My love for thee doth take me unaware,
  When most with lesser things my brain is wrought,
  As in some nimble interchange of thought
The silence enters, and the talkers stare.
Suddenly I am still and thou art there,
  A viewless visitant and unbesought,
  And all my thinking trembles into nought
And all my being opens like a prayer.
Thou art the lifted Chalice in my soul,
  And I a dim church at the thought of thee;
    Brief be the moment, but the mass is said,
The benediction like an aureole
  Is on my spirit, and shuddering through me
    A rapture like the rapture of the dead.

RICHARD HOVEY
[1864–1900]

LOVE'S SPRINGTIDE

My heart was winter-bound until
  I heard you sing;
O voice of Love, hush not, but fill
  My life with Spring!

My hopes were homeless things before
  I saw your eyes;
O smile of Love, close not the door
  To paradise!

My dreams were bitter once, and then
  I found them bliss;
O lips of Love, give me again
  Your rose to kiss!

Springtide of Love! The secret sweet
  Is ours alone;
O heart of Love, at last you beat
  Against my own!

FRANK DEMPSTER SHERMAN
[1860–1916]

SUMMER

Come we to the summer, to the summer we will
       come,
For the woods are full of bluebells and the hedges full
       of bloom,
And the crow is on the oak a-building of her nest,
And love is burning diamonds in my true lover's
       breast;
She sits beneath the whitethorn a-plaiting of her hair,
And I will to my true lover with a fond request repair;
I will look upon her face, I will in her beauty rest,
And lay my aching weariness upon her lovely breast.

The clock-a-clay is creeping on the open bloom of
       May,
The merry bee is trampling the pinky threads all day,
And the chaffinch it is brooding on its grey mossy nest
In the whitethorn bush where I will lean upon my
       lover's breast;
I'll lean upon her breast and I'll whisper in her ear
That I cannot get a wink o'sleep for thinking of my
       dear;
I hunger at my meat and I daily fade away
Like the hedge rose that is broken in the heat of the
       day.

JOHN CLARE
[1793–1864]

22

THE LOOK

Strephon kissed me in the spring,
   Robin in the fall,
But Colin only looked at me
   And never kissed at all.

Strephon's kiss was lost in jest,
   Robin's lost in play,
But the kiss in Colin's eyes
   Haunts me night and day.

SARA TEASDALE
[1884–1933]

———

VALENTINES
(written for Miss L——'s Valentine Parties)

To ——.

We never met; yet to my soul
Thy name hath been a voice of singing,
And ever to thy glorious lays
The echoes of my heart are ringing.

We never met; yet is thy face,
Thy pictured face, before me now;
Strangely, like life, I almost see
The dark curls wave upon thy brow!

This face reveals that poet-life,
Still deepening, still rising higher,
A breathing from thy soul of song,
A glow from out thy heart of fire!

And yet, unlike thy portraiture
I would thy *living* face might be,
For ever, as I gaze on *this*,
Thine eyes are turned away from me.

GRACE GREENWOOD
[1823–1904]

THE FAIR SINGER

To make a final conquest of all me,
Love did compose so sweet an enemy,
In whom both beauties to my death agree,
Joining themselves in fatal harmony;
That while she with her eyes my heart does bind,
She with her voice might captivate my mind.

I could have fled from one but singly fair,
My disentangled soul itself might save,
Breaking the curled trammels of her hair.
But how should I avoid to be her slave,
Whose subtle art invisibly can wreath
My fetters of the very air I breathe?

It had been easy fighting in some plain,
Where victory might hang in equal choice,
But all resistance against her is vain,
Who has th'advantage both of eyes and voice,
And all my forces needs must be undone,
She having gained both the wind and sun.

ANDREW MARVELL
[1621–1678]

SUDDEN LIGHT

I have been here before,
　　But when or how I cannot tell:
I know the grass beyond the door,
　　The sweet keen smell,
The sighing sound, the lights around the shore.

You have been mine before,—
　　How long ago I may not know:
But just when at that swallow's soar
　　Your neck turn'd so,
Some veil did fall,—I knew it all of yore.

Has this been thus before?
　　And shall not thus time's eddying flight
Still with our lives our love restore
　　In death's despite,
And day and night yield one delight once more?

DANTE GABRIEL ROSSETTI
[1828–1882]

AIR AND ANGELS

Twice or thrice had I lov'd thee,
Before I knew thy face or name;
So in a voice, so in a shapeless flame
Angels affect us oft, and worshipp'd be;
  Still when, to where thou wert, I came,
Some lovely glorious nothing I did see.
  But since my soul, whose child love is,
Takes limbs of flesh, and else could nothing do,
  More subtle than the parent is
Love must not be, but take a body too;
  And therefore what thou wert, and who,
    I bid Love ask, and now
That it assume thy body, I allow,
And fix itself in thy lip, eye, and brow.

Whilst thus to ballast love I thought,
And so more steadily to have gone,
With wares which would sink admiration,
I saw I had love's pinnace overfraught;
  Ev'ry thy hair for love to work upon
Is much too much, some fitter must be sought;
  For, nor in nothing, nor in things
Extreme, and scatt'ring bright, can love inhere;
  Then, as an angel, face, and wings
Of air, not pure as it, yet pure, doth wear,
  So thy love may be my love's sphere;

        Just such disparity
As is 'twixt air and angels' purity,
'Twixt women's love, and men's, will ever be.

JOHN DONNE
[1573–1631]

THE DEFINITION OF LOVE

My love is of a birth as rare
As 'tis for object strange and high;
It was begotten by Despair
Upon Impossibility.

Magnanimous Despair alone
Could show me so divine a thing
Where feeble Hope could ne'er have flown,
But vainly flapp'd its tinsel wing.

And yet I quickly might arrive
Where my extended soul is fixt,
But Fate does iron wedges drive,
And always crowds itself betwixt.

For Fate with jealous eye does see
Two perfect loves, nor lets them close;
Their union would her ruin be,
And her tyrannic pow'r depose.

And therefore her decrees of steel
Us as the distant poles have plac'd,
(Though love's whole world on us doth wheel)
Not by themselves to be embrac'd;

Unless the giddy heaven fall,
And earth some new convulsion tear;

And, us to join, the world should all
Be cramp'd into a planisphere.

As lines, so loves oblique may well
Themselves in every angle greet;
But ours so truly parallel,
Though infinite, can never meet.

Therefore the love which us doth bind,
But Fate so enviously debars,
Is the conjunction of the mind,
And opposition of the stars.

ANDREW MARVELL
[1621–1678]

———

30

ABSENT YET PRESENT

As the flight of a river
   That flows to the sea
My soul rushes ever
   In tumult to thee.

A twofold existence
   I am where thou art:
My heart in the distance
   Beats close to thy heart.

Look up, I am near thee,
   I gaze on thy face:
I see thee, I hear thee,
   I feel thine embrace.

As the magnet's control on
   The steel it draws to it,
Is the charm of thy soul on
   The thoughts that pursue it.

And absence but brightens
   The eyes that I miss,
And custom but heightens
   The spell of thy kiss.

It is not from duty,
   Though that may be owed,—

It is not from beauty,
Though that be bestowed:

But all that I care for,
And all that I know,
Is that, without wherefore,
I worship thee so.

Through granite it breaketh
A tree to the ray:
As a dreamer forsaketh
The grief of the day,

My soul in its fever
Escapes unto thee:
O dream to the griever!
O light to the tree!

A twofold existence
I am where thou art:
Hark, hear in the distance
The beat of my heart!

EDWARD BULWER-LYTTON
[1805–1873]

———

LOVE

*L*ove bade me welcome; yet my soul drew back,
　　Guilty of dust and sin.
But quick-eyed Love, observing me grow slack
　　From my first entrance in,
Drew nearer to me, sweetly questioning
　　If I lacked anything.

"A guest," I answered, "worthy to be here";
　　Love said, "You shall be he."
"I, the unkind, ungrateful? Ah, my dear,
　　I cannot look on Thee."
Love took my hand, and smiling did reply,
　　"Who made the eyes but I?"

"Truth, Lord, but I have marred them; let my shame
　　Go where it doth deserve."
"And know you not," says Love, "who bore the
　　　　blame?"
　　"My dear, then I will serve."
"You must sit down," says Love, "and taste My meat."
　　So I did sit and eat.

GEORGE HERBERT
[1593–1633]

A BIRTHDAY

y heart is like a singing bird
Whose nest is in a water'd shoot;
My heart is like an apple-tree
Whose boughs are bent with thickset fruit;
My heart is like a rainbow shell
That paddles in a halcyon sea;
My heart is gladder than all these
Because my love is come to me.

Raise me a dais of silk and down;
Hang it with vair and purple dyes;
Carve it in doves and pomegranates,
And peacocks with a hundred eyes;
Work it in gold and silver grapes,
In leaves and silver fleurs-de-lys;
Because the birthday of my life
Is come, my love is come to me.

CHRISTINA ROSSETTI
[1830–1894]

JENNY KISSED ME

Jenny kissed me when we met,
  Jumping from the chair she sat in.
Time, you thief! who love to get
  Sweets into your list, put that in.
Say I'm weary, say I'm sad;
  Say that health and wealth have missed me;
Say I'm growing old, but add—
          Jenny kissed me!

LEIGH HUNT
[1784–1859]

35

A SONG:
WHEN JUNE IS PAST, THE FADING ROSE

Ask me no more where Jove bestows,
When June is past, the fading rose;
For in your beauty's orient deep
These flowers as in their causes, sleep.

Ask me no more whither doth stray
The golden atoms of the day;
For in pure love heaven did prepare
Those powders to enrich your hair.

Ask me no more whither doth haste
The nightingale, when May is past;
For in your sweet dividing throat
She winters and keeps warm her note.

Ask me no more where those stars' light
That downwards fall in dead of night;
For in your eyes they sit, and there,
Fixèd become, as in their sphere.

Ask me no more if east or west
The phœnix builds her spicy nest;
For unto you at last she flies,
And in your fragrant bosom dies.

THOMAS CAREW
[1595?–1640]

I LIVED WITH VISIONS

I lived with visions for my company,
Instead of men and women, years ago,
And found them gentle mates, nor thought to know
A sweeter music than they played to me.
But soon their trailing purple was not free
Of this world's dust,—their lutes did silent grow,
And I myself grew faint and blind below
Their vanishing eyes. Then THOU didst come . . .
        to be,
Belovèd, what they seemed. Their shining fronts,
Their songs, their splendours, (better, yet the same,
As river-water hallowed into fonts)
Met in thee, and from out thee overcame
My soul with satisfaction of all wants—
Because God's gifts put man's best dreams to shame.

ELIZABETH BARRETT BROWNING
[1806–1861]

THE STRING AROUND MY FINGER

The bell that strikes the warning hour,
Reminds me that I should not linger,
And winds around my heart its power,
Tight as the string around my finger.

A sweet good-night I give, and then
Far from my thoughts I need must fling her,
Who blessed that lovely evening, when
She tied the string around my finger.

Lovely and virtuous, kind and fair,
A sweet-toned bell, O! who shall ring her!
Of her let bell men all beware,
Who ties such strings around their finger.

What shall I do?—I'll sit me down,
And, in my leisure hours, I'll sing her
Who gave me neither smile nor frown,
But tied a thread around my finger.

Now may the quiet star-lit hours
Their gentlest dews and perfumes bring her;
And morning show its sweetest flowers
To her whose string is round my finger.

And never more may I forget
The spot where I so long did linger;—
But watch another chance, and get
Another string around my finger.

JOHN BRAINARD
[1796–1828]

ON A GIRDLE

That which her slender waist confin'd,
Shall now my joyful temples bind;
No monarch but would give his crown,
His arms might do what this has done.

It was my heaven's extremest sphere,
The pale which held that lovely deer,
My joy, my grief, my hope, my love,
Did all within this circle move.

A narrow compass, and yet there
Dwelt all that's good, and all that's fair;
Give me but what this ribbon bound,
Take all the rest the sun goes 'round.

EDMUND WALLER
[1606–1687]

GIVE ALL TO LOVE

*G*ive all to love;
Obey thy heart;
Friends, kindred, days,
Estate, good fame,
Plans, credit, and the muse;
Nothing refuse.

'Tis a brave master,
Let it have scope,
Follow it utterly,
Hope beyond hope;
High and more high,
It dives into noon,
With wing unspent,
Untold intent;
But 'tis a god,
Knows its own path,
And the outlets of the sky.

'Tis not for the mean,
It requireth courage stout,
Souls above doubt,
Valor unbending;
Such 'twill reward,
They shall return
More than they were,
And ever ascending.

Leave all for love;—
Yet, hear me, yet,
One word more thy heart behoved,
One pulse more of firm endeavor,
Keep thee to-day,
To-morrow, for ever,
Free as an Arab
Of thy beloved.
Cling with life to the maid;
But when the surprise,
Vague shadow of surmise,
Flits across her bosom young
Of a joy apart from thee,
Free be she, fancy-free,
Do not thou detain a hem,

Nor the palest rose she flung
From her summer diadem.

Though thou loved her as thyself,
As a self of purer clay,
Tho' her parting dims the day,
Stealing grace from all alive,
Heartily know,
When half-gods go,
The gods arrive.

RALPH WALDO EMERSON
[1803–1882]

————

42

LOVE ME NOT FOR COMELY GRACE

_L_ove not me for comely grace,
For my pleasing eye or face;
Nor for any outward part,
No, nor for my constant heart:
　For those may fail or turn to ill,
　So thou and I shall sever.
Keep therefore a true woman's eye,
And love me still, but know not why;
　So hast thou the same reason still
　To doat upon me ever.

JOHN WILBYE
[1574–1638]

———

MEETING AT NIGHT

I

The grey sea and the long black land;
And the yellow half-moon large and low;
And the startled little waves that leap
In fiery ringlets from their sleep,
As I gain the cove with pushing prow,
And quench its speed i' the slushy sand.

II

Then a mile of warm sea-scented beach;
Three fields to cross till a farm appears;
A tap at the pane, the quick sharp scratch
And blue spurt of a lighted match,
And a voice less loud, thro' its joys and fears,
Than the two hearts beating each to each!

ROBERT BROWNING
[1812–1889]

─────────

SONG TO AMARANTHA,
THAT SHE WOULD DISHEVEL HER HAIR

Amarantha sweet and fair
Ah braid no more that shining hair!
　As my curious hand or eye
Hovering round thee let it fly.

　Let it fly as unconfin'd
As its calm ravisher, the wind,
　Who hath left his darling th'East,
To wanton o'er that spicy nest.

　Ev'ry tress must be confest
But neatly tangled at the best;
　Like a clue of golden thread,
Most excellently ravelled.

　Do not then wind up that light
In ribands, and o'er-cloud in night;
　Like the sun in's early ray,
But shake your head and scatter day.

　See 'tis broke! Within this grove
The bower, and the walks of love,
　Weary lie we down and rest,
And fan each other's panting breast.

Here we'll strip and cool our fire
In cream below, in milk-baths higher:
  And when all wells are drawn dry,
I'll drink a tear out of thine eye,

  Which our very joys shall leave
That sorrows thus we can deceive;
  Or our very sorrows weep,
That joys so ripe, so little keep.

RICHARD LOVELACE
[1618–1657]

SHE WALKS IN BEAUTY

She walks in beauty, like the night
Of cloudless climes and starry skies;
And all that's best of dark and bright
Meet in her aspect and her eyes:
Thus mellow'd to that tender light
Which heaven to gaudy day denies.

One shade the more, one ray the less,
Had half impair'd the nameless grace
Which waves in every raven tress,
Or softly lightens o'er her face;
Where thoughts serenely sweet express
How pure, how dear their dwelling-place.

And on that cheek, and o'er that brow,
So soft, so calm, yet eloquent,
The smiles that win, the tints that glow,
But tell of days in goodness spent,
A mind at peace with all below,
A heart whose love is innocent!

LORD BYRON
[1788–1824]

———

MY STAR

All that I know
Of a certain star,
Is, it can throw
(Like the angled spar)
Now a dart of red,
Now a dart of blue,
Till my friends have said
They would fain see, too,
My star that dartles the red and the blue!

Then it stops like a bird; like a flower, hangs furled:
    They must solace themselves with the Saturn above it.
What matter to me if their star is a world?
    Mine has opened its soul to me; therefore I love it.

ROBERT BROWNING
[1812–1889]

———

DESIRE

Where true Love burns Desire is Love's pure flame;
It is the reflex of our earthly frame,
That takes its meaning from the nobler part,
And but translates the language of the heart.

SAMUEL TAYLOR COLERIDGE
[1772–1834]

THE LOVE I BEAR THEE

And wilt thou have me fashion into speech
The love I bear thee, finding words enough,
And hold the torch out, while the winds are rough,
Between our faces, to cast light on each?—
I drop it at thy feet. I cannot teach
My hand to hold my spirit so far off
From myself—me—that I should bring thee proof
In words, of love hid in me out of reach.
Nay, let the silence of my womanhood
Commend my woman-love to thy belief,—
Seeing that I stand unwon, however wooed,
And rend the garment of my life, in brief,
By a most dauntless, voiceless fortitude,
Lest one touch of this heart convey its grief.

ELIZABETH BARRETT BROWNING
[1770–1850]

SUNDAY UP THE RIVER
(excerpt)

Give a man a horse he can ride,
  Give a man a boat he can sail;
And his rank and wealth, his strength and health,
  On sea nor shore shall fail.

Give a man a pipe he can smoke,
  Give a man a book he can read;
And his home is bright with a calm delight,
  Though the room be poor indeed.

Give a man a girl he can love,
  As I, O my Love, love thee;
And his heart is great with the pulse of Fate,
  At home, on land, on sea.

JAMES THOMSON
[1834–1882]

THE KISS

Before you kissed me only winds of heaven
Had kissed me, and the tenderness of rain—
Now you have come, how can I care for kisses
Like theirs again?

I sought the sea, she sent her winds to meet me,
They surged about me singing of the south—
I turned my head away to keep still holy
Your kiss upon my mouth.

And swift sweet rains of shining April weather
Found not my lips where living kisses are;
I bowed my head lest they put out my glory
As rain puts out a star.

I am my love's and he is mine forever,
Sealed with a seal and safe forevermore—
Think you that I could let a beggar enter
Where a king stood before?

ON A FAIR MORNING,
AS I CAME BY THE WAY

*O*n a fair morning, as I came by the way,
Met I with a merry maid in the merry month of May,
When a sweet love sings his lovely lay,
And every bird upon the bush bechirps it up so gay.
With a heave and ho! with a heave and ho!
Thy wife shall be thy master, I trow.
Sing care away, care away, let the world go!
Hey, lustily, all in a row, all in a row,
Sing care away, care away, let the world go!

THOMAS MORLEY
[1557–1602]

———

THE WINE OF LOVE

The wine of Love is music,
  And the feast of Love is song:
And when Love sits down to the banquet,
  Love sits long:

 Sits long and ariseth drunken,
  But not with the feast and the wine;
He reeleth with his own heart,
  That great rich Vine.

JAMES THOMSON
[1834–1882]

II

Dreams
of the
Future

TO CELIA

Not, Celia, that I juster am,
  Or better than the rest;
For I would change each hour like them
  Were not my heart at rest.

But I am tied to very thee,
  By every thought I have;
Thy face I only care to see,
  Thy heart I only crave.

All that in woman is ador'd
  In thy dear self I find;
For the whole sex can but afford
  The handsome and the kind.

Why then should I seek farther store
  And still make love anew?
When change itself can give no more,
  'Tis easy to be true.

SIR CHARLES SEDLEY
[1639?–1701]

WEDDING PRAYER

*N*ow you will feel no rain,
  For each of you will be shelter to the other.
Now you will feel no cold,
  For each of you will be warmth to the other.
Now there is no more loneliness,
  For each of you will be companion to the other.
Now you are two bodies,
  But there is only one life before you.
Go now to your dwelling place
  To enter into the days of your togetherness
And may your days be good and long upon the earth.

TRADITIONAL APACHE PRAYER
[*date unknown*]

———

I WILL MAKE YOU BROOCHES

❁

I will make you brooches and toys for your delight
Of bird-song at morning and star-shine at night.
I will make a palace fit for you and me
Of green days in forests and blue days at sea.

I will make my kitchen, and you shall keep your room,
Where white flows the river and bright blows the
      broom,
And you shall wash your linen and keep your body
      white
In rainfall at morning and dewfall at night.

And this shall be for music when no one else is near,
The fine song for singing, the rare song to hear!
That only I remember, that only you admire,
Of the broad road that stretches and the roadside fire.

ROBERT LOUIS STEVENSON
[1850–1894]

TO CELIA

Drink to me only with thine eyes,
 And I will pledge with mine;
Or leave a kiss but in the cup
 And I'll not look for wine.
The thirst that from the soul doth rise
 Doth ask a drink divine;
But might I of Jove's nectar sup,
 I would not change for thine.

I set thee late a rosy wreath,
 Not so much honouring thee
As giving it a hope that there
 It could not withered be;
But thou thereon didst only breathe
 And sent'st it back to me;
Since when it grows, and smells, I swear
 Not of itself but thee!

BEN JONSON
[1573–1637]

BEAUTY THAT IS NEVER OLD

*W*hen buffeted and beaten by life's storms,
When by the bitter cares of life oppressed,
I want no surer haven than your arms,
I want no sweeter heaven than your breast.

When over my life's way there falls the blight
Of sunless days, and nights of starless skies;
Enough for me, the calm and steadfast light
That softly shines within your loving eyes.

The world, for me, and all the world can hold
Is circled by your arms; for me there lies,
Within the lights and shadows of your eyes,
The only beauty that is never old.

JAMES WELDON JOHNSON
[1871–1938]

SONG

❀

I saw thee on thy bridal day—
    When a burning blush came o'er thee,
Though happiness around thee lay,
    The world all love before thee:

And in thine eye a kindling light
    (Whatever it might be)
Was all on Earth my aching sight
    Of Loveliness could see.

That blush, perhaps, was maiden shame—
    As such it well may pass—
Though its glow hath raised a fiercer flame
    In the breast of him, alas!

Who saw thee on that bridal day,
    When that deep blush *would* come o'er thee,
Though happiness around thee lay,
    The world all love before thee.

EDGAR ALLAN POE
[1809–1849]

COME, MY CELIA

Come, my celia, let us prove
While we may, the sports of love;
Time will not be ours forever;
He at length our good will sever.
Spend not then his gifts in vain.
Suns that set may rise again;
But if once we lose this light,
'Tis with us perpetual night.
Why should we defer our joys?
Fame and rumor are but toys.
Cannot we delude the eyes
Of a few poor household spies,
Or his easier ears beguile,
So removed by our wile?
'Tis no sin love's fruit to steal;
But the sweet theft to reveal.
To be taken, to be seen,
These have crimes accounted been.

BEN JONSON
[1573–1637]

MOST SWEET IT IS

Most sweet it is with unuplifted eyes
To pace the ground, if path be there or none,
While a fair region 'round the traveller lies
Which he forbears again to look upon;
Pleased rather with some soft ideal scene,
The work of Fancy, or some happy tone
Of meditation, slipping in between
The beauty coming and the beauty gone.
If Thought and Love desert us, from that day
Let us break off all commerce with the Muse:
With Thought and Love companions of our way,
Whate'er the senses take or may refuse,
The Mind's internal heaven shall shed her dews
Of inspiration on the humblest lay.

WILLIAM WORDSWORTH
[1770–1850]

SHALL I COMPARE THEE

Shall I compare thee to a summer's day?
Thou art more lovely and more temperate:
Rough winds do shake the darling buds of May;
And summer's lease hath all too short a date.
Sometime too hot the eye of heaven shines,
And often is his gold complexion dimm'd;
And every fair from fair sometime declines,
By chance or nature's changing course untrimm'd;
But thy eternal summer shall not fade,
Nor lose possession of that fair thou owest;
Nor shall Death brag thou wand'rest in his shade,
When in eternal lines to time thou growest:
    So long as men can breathe or eyes can see,
    So long lives this, and this gives life to thee.

WILLIAM SHAKESPEARE
[1564–1616]

LOVE THYSELF LAST

*L*ove thyself last. Look near, behold thy duty
To those who walk beside thee down life's road;
Make glad their days by little acts of beauty,
And them bear the burden of earth's load.

Love thyself last. Look far and find the stranger,
Who staggers 'neath his sin and his despair;
Go lend a hand, and lead him out of danger,
To heights where he may see the world is fair.

Love thyself last. The vastnesses above thee
Are filled with Spirit Forces, strong and pure.
And fervently, these faithful friends shall love thee:
Keep thou thy watch o'er others, and endure.

Love thyself last; and oh, such joy shall thrill thee,
As never yet to selfish souls was given.
Whate'er thy lot, a perfect peace will fill thee,
And earth shall seem the ante-room of Heaven.

Love thyself last, and thou shall grow in spirit
To see, to hear, to know, and understand.
The message of the stars, lo, thou shall hear it,
And all God's joys shall be at thy command.

ELLA WHEELER WILCOX
[1850–1919]

TO ANTHEA,
WHO MAY COMMAND HIM ANYTHING

*B*id me to live, and I will live
 Thy protestant to be;
Or bid me love, and I will give
 A loving heart to thee.

A heart as soft, a heart as kind,
 A heart as sound and free,
As in the whole world thou canst find,
 That heart I'll give to thee.

Bid that heart stay, and it will stay,
 To honour thy decree;
Or bid it languish quite away,
 And 't shall do so for thee.

Bid me to weep, and I will weep,
 While I have eyes to see;
And having none, yet I will keep
 A heart to weep for thee.

Bid me despair, and I'll despair,
 Under that cypress tree;
Or bid me die, and I will dare
 E'en death, to die for thee.

Thou art my life, my love, my heart,
    The very eyes of me;
And hast command of every part,
    To live and die for thee.

ROBERT HERRICK
[1591–1674]

DON'T TELL THE WORLD
THAT YOU'RE WAITING FOR ME

Three summers have gone since the first time we
     met, love,
  And still 'tis in vain that I ask thee to wed;
I hear no reply but a gentle "Not yet, love,"
  With a smile of your lip, and a shake of your head.
Ah! how oft have I whispered, how oft have I sued
      thee,
  And breathed my soul's question of "When shall it
     be?"
You know, dear, how long and how truly I've wooed
     thee,
  So don't tell the world that you're waiting for me.

I have fashioned a home, where the fairies might
     dwell, love,
  I've planted the myrtle, the rose, and the vine;
But the cottage to me is a mere hermit's cell, love,
  And the bloom will be dull till the flowers are thine.
I've a ring of bright gold, which I gaze on when
     lonely,
  And sigh with Hope's eloquence, "When will it be?"
There needs but thy "Yes," love—one little word only,
  So don't tell the world that you're waiting for me.

ELIZA COOK
[1818–1889]

———

MY DEAR AND ONLY LOVE

My dear and only Love, I pray
   This noble world of thee
Be govern'd by no other sway
   But purest monarchy;
For if confusion have a part,
   Which virtuous souls abhor,
And hold a synod in thy heart,
   I'll never love thee more.

Like Alexander I will reign,
   And I will reign alone,
My thoughts shall evermore disdain
   A rival on my throne.
He either fears his fate too much,
   Or his deserts are small,
That puts it not unto the touch
   To win or lose it all.

But I must rule and govern still,
   And always give the law,
And have each subject at my will,
   And all to stand in awe.
But 'gainst my battery, if I find
   Thou shunn'st the prize so sore
As that thou sett'st me up a blind,
   I'll never love thee more.

Or in the empire of thy heart,
  Where I should solely be,
Another do pretend a part
  And dares to vie with me;
Or if committees thou erect,
  And go on such a score,
I'll sing and laugh at thy neglect,
  And never love thee more.

But if thou wilt be constant then,
  And faithful of thy word,
I'll make thee glorious by my pen
  And famous by my sword:
I'll serve thee in such noble ways
  Was never heard before;
I'll crown and deck thee all with bays,
  And love thee evermore.

JAMES GRAHAM, MARQUIS OF MONTROSE
[1612–1650]

A PRAISE OF HIS LOVE

*G*ive place, ye lovers, here before
That spent your boasts and brags it vain;
My lady's beauty passeth more
The best of yours, I dare well sayn,
Than doth the sun the candle-light,
Or brightest day the darkest night.

And thereto hath a troth as just
As had Penelope the fair;
For what she saith, ye may it trust,
As it by writing sealèd were;
And virtues hath she many mo
Than I with pen have skill to show.

I could rehearse, if that I wold,
The whole effect of Nature's plaint,
When she had lost the perfit mould,
The like to whom she could not paint;
With wringing hands, how she did cry,
And what she said, I know it, I.

I know she swore with raging mind,
Her kingdom only set apart,
There was no loss by law of kind,
That could have gone so near her heart;
And this was chiefly all her pain;
She could not make the like again.

Sith Nature thus gave her the praise,
To be the chiefest work she wrought;
In faith, methink, some better ways
On your behalf might well be sought,
Than to compare, as ye have done,
To match the candle with the sun.

HENRY HOWARD, EARL OF SURREY
[1517–1547]

THE PASSIONATE SHEPHERD
TO HIS LOVE

Come live with me and be my love,
And we will all the pleasures prove,
That valleys, groves, hills, and fields,
Woods, or steepy mountain yields.

And we will sit upon the rocks,
Seeing the shepherds feed their flocks,
By shallow rivers, to whose falls
Melodious birds sing madrigals.

And I will make thee beds of roses,
And a thousand fragrant posies,
A cap of flowers and a kirtle
Embroider'd all with leaves of myrtle.

A gown made of the finest wool,
Which from our pretty lambs we pull;
Fair linèd slippers for the cold,
With buckles of the purest gold.

A belt of straw and ivy buds,
With coral clasps and amber studs:
And if these pleasures may thee move,
Come live with me and be my love.

The shepherd swains shall dance and sing
For thy delight each May morning:
If these delights thy mind may move,
Then live with me and be my love.

CHRISTOPHER MARLOWE
[1564–1593]

THE NYMPH'S REPLY TO THE SHEPHERD

Of all the world and love were young,
And truth in every shepherd's tongue,
These pretty pleasures might me move
To live with thee and be thy love.

Time drives the flocks from field to fold,
When rivers rage and rocks grow cold,
And Philomel becometh dumb;
The rest complains of cares to come.

The flowers do fade, and wanton fields
To wayward winter reckoning yields;
A honey tongue, a heart of gall,
Is fancy's spring, but sorrow's fall.

Thy gowns, thy shoes, thy beds of roses,
Thy cap, thy kirtle, and thy posies
Soon break, soon wither, soon forgotten,—
In folly ripe, in reason rotten.

Thy belt of straw and ivy buds,
The coral clasps and amber studs,
All these in me no means can move
To come to thee and be thy love.

But could youth last and love still breed,
Had joys no date nor age no need,
Then these delights my mind might move
To live with thee and be thy love.

SIR WALTER RALEIGH
[1552–1618]

IF THOU MUST LOVE ME

Of thou must love me, let it be for nought
Except for love's sake only. Do not say
"I love her for her smile . . . her look . . . her way
Of speaking gently, . . . for a trick of thought
That falls in well with mine, and certes brought
A sense of pleasant ease on such a day"—
For these things in themselves, Beloved, may
Be changed, or change for thee,—and love, so
      wrought,
May be unwrought so. Neither love me for
Thine own dear pity's wiping my cheeks dry,
A creature might forget to weep who bore
Thy comfort long, and lose thy love thereby.
But love me for love's sake, that evermore
Thou may'st love on, through love's eternity.

ELIZABETH BARRETT BROWNING
[1806–1861]

LOVE IS ENOUGH: SONG I

*L*ove is enough: though the World be a-waning,
And the woods have no voice but the voice of
      complaining,
  Though the sky be too dark for dim eyes to discover
The gold-cups and daisies fair blooming thereunder,
Though the hills be held shadows, and the sea a dark
      wonder,
  And this day draw a veil over all deeds pass'd over,
Yet their hands shall not tremble, their feet shall not
      falter:
The void shall not weary, the fear shall not alter
  These lips and these eyes of the loved and the lover.

WILLIAM MORRIS
[1834–1896]

TO JANE

The keen stars were twinkling,
And the fair moon was rising among them,
     Dear Jane.
The guitar was tinkling,
  But the notes were not sweet till you sung them
     Again.

  As the moon's soft splendour
O'er the faint cold starlight of Heaven
     Is thrown,
  So your voice most tender
To the strings without soul had then given
     Its own.

  The stars will awaken,
Though the moon sleep a full hour later
     To-night;
  No leaf will be shaken
Whilst the dews of your melody scatter
     Delight.

  Though the sound overpowers,
Sing again, with your dear voice revealing
     A tone

Of some world far from ours,
Where music and moonlight and feeling
Are one.

PERCY BYSSHE SHELLEY
[1792–1822]

AFTER PARTING

Oh I have sown my love so wide
That he will find it everywhere;
It will awake him in the night,
It will enfold him in the air.

I set my shadow in his sight
And I have winged it with desire,
That it may be a cloud by day
And in the night a shaft of fire.

SARA TEASDALE
[1884–1933]

WHEN, DEAREST, I BUT THINK ON THEE

When, dearest, I but think on thee,
Methinks all things that lovely be
Are present, and my soul delighted:
   For beauties that from worth arise
   Are like the grace of deities,
Still present with us, though unsighted.

  Thus while I sit and sigh the day
With all his spreading lights away,
Till night's black wings do overtake me:
   Thinking on thee, thy beauties then,
   As sudden lights do sleeping men,
So they by their bright rays awake me.

  Thus absence dies, and dying proves
No absence can consist with loves
That do partake of fair perfection:
   Since in the darkest night they may
   By their quick motion find a way
To see each other by reflection.

  The waving sea can with such flood
Bathe some high palace that hath stood

Far from the main up in the river:
    Oh think not then but love can do
    As much, for that's an ocean too,
That flows not every day, but ever.

OWEN FELLTHAM
[1602?–1668]

HOW DO I LOVE THEE?

How do I love thee? Let me count the ways.
I love thee to the depth and breadth and height
My soul can reach, when feeling out of sight
For the ends of Being and ideal Grace.
I love thee to the level of every day's
Most quiet need, by sun and candlelight.
I love thee freely, as men strive for Right;
I love thee purely, as they turn from Praise.
I love thee with the passion put to use
In my old griefs, and with my childhood's faith.
I love thee with a love I seemed to lose
With my lost saints,—I love thee with the breath,
Smiles, tears, of all my life!—and, if God choose,
I shall but love thee better after death.

ELIZABETH BARRETT BROWNING
[1806–1861]

III

*A
Life
Together*

MUSIC, WHEN SOFT VOICES DIE

Music, when soft voices die,
Vibrates in the memory—
Odours, when sweet violets sicken,
Live within the sense they quicken.

Rose leaves, when the rose is dead,
Are heap'd for the beloved's bed;
And so thy thoughts, when thou art gone,
Love itself shall slumber on.

PERCY BYSSHE SHELLEY
[1792–1822]

LOVE'S CALENDAR

The Summer comes and the Summer goes;
Wild-flowers are fringing the dusty lanes,
The swallows go darting through fragrant rains,
Then, all of a sudden—it snows.

Dear Heart, our lives so happily flow,
So lightly we heed the flying hours,
We only know Winter is gone—by the flowers,
We only know Winter is come—by the snow.

THOMAS BAILEY ALDRICH
[1836–1907]

ART

(excerpt)

❀

"What precious thing are you making fast
    In all these silken lines?
And where and to whom will it go at last?
    Such subtle knots and twines!"

"I am tying up all my love in this,
    With all its hopes and fears,
With all its anguish and all its bliss,
    And its hours as heavy as years.

"I am going to send it afar, afar,
    To I know not where above;
To that sphere beyond the highest star
    Where dwells the soul of my Love.

"But in vain, in vain, would I make it fast
    With countless subtle twines;
Forever its fire breaks out at last,
    And shrivels all the lines."

JAMES THOMSON
[1834–1882]

———

LOVE IS LOVE

The lowest trees have tops, the ant her gall,
  The fly her spleen, the little sparks their heat;
The slender hairs cast shadows, though but small,
  And bees have stings, although they be not great;
Seas have their source, and so have shallow springs;
And love is love, in beggars as in kings.

Where rivers smoothest run, deep are the fords;
  The dial stirs, yet none perceives it move;
The firmest faith is in the fewest words;
  The turtles cannot sing, and yet they love:
True hearts have eyes and ears, no tongues to speak;
They hear and see, and sigh, and then they break.

SIR EDWARD DYER
[1550?–1607]

THE MARRIAGE OF TRUE MINDS

*L*et me not to the marriage of true minds
Admit impediments; love is not love
Which alters when it alteration finds,
Or bends with the remover to remove.
Oh, no, it is an ever-fixèd mark
That looks on tempests and is never shaken;
It is the star to every wand'ring bark,
Whose worth's unknown, although his height be
      taken.
Love's not Time's fool, though rosy lips and cheeks
Within his bending sickle's compass come;
Love alters not with his brief hours and weeks,
But bears it out even to the edge of Doom.
  If this be error and upon me proved,
  I never writ, nor no man ever loved.

WILLIAM SHAKESPEARE
[1564–1616]

LOVE'S EMBLEMS

There was a rose, that blushing grew
Within my life's young bower;
The angels sprinkled holy dew
Upon the blessed flower.
I glory to resign it, love,
Though it was dear to me;
Amid thy laurels twine it, love,
It only blooms for thee.

There was a rich and radiant gem
I long kept hid from sight;
Lost from some seraph's diadem,
It shone with heaven's own light!
The world could never tear it, love,
That gem of gems, from me;
Yet on thy fond breast wear it, love,
It only shines for thee.

There was a bird came to my breast,
When I was very young;
I only knew that sweet bird's nest,
To me she only sung.
But, ah! one summer day, love,
I saw that bird depart!
The truant flew thy way, love,
And nestled in thy heart!

GRACE GREENWOOD
[1823–1904]

————

SONG

❁

How many times do I love thee, dear?
  Tell me how many thoughts there be
      In the atmosphere
      Of a new-fall'n year,
Whose white and sable hours appear
  The latest flake of Eternity:—
So many times do I love thee, dear.

How many times do I love again?
  Tell me how many beads there are
      In a silver chain
      Of evening rain,
Unravelled from the tumbling main,
  And threading the eye of a yellow star:—
So many times do I love again.

THOMAS LOVELL BEDDOES
[1803–1849]

———

95

TO F——

Beloved! amid the earnest woes
   That crowd around my earthly path—
(Drear path, alas! where grows
Not even one lonely rose)—
   My soul at least a solace hath
In dreams of thee, and therein knows
An Eden of bland repose.

And thus thy memory is to me
   Like some enchanted far-off isle
In some tumultuous sea—
Some ocean throbbing far and free
   With storms—but where meanwhile
Serenest skies continually
   Just o'er that one bright island smile.

EDGAR ALLAN POE
[1809–1849]

DELIA

(34)

*W*hen winter snows upon thy golden hairs,
And frost of age hath nipped thy flowers near;
When dark shall seem thy day that never clears,
And all lies with'red that was held so dear;
Then take this picture which I here present thee,
Limned with a pencil not all unworthy.
Here see the gifts that God and nature lent thee;
Here read thy self and what I suff'red for thee.
This may remain thy lasting monument,
Which happily posterity may cherish.
These colors with thy fading are not spent;
These may remain when thou and I shall perish.
If they remain, then thou shalt live thereby:
They will remain, and so thou canst not die.

SAMUEL DANIEL
[1562–1619]

———

SHE WAS A PHANTOM OF DELIGHT

She was a Phantom of delight
When first she gleamed upon my sight;
A lovely Apparition, sent
To be a moment's ornament;
Her eyes as stars of Twilight fair;
Like Twilight's, too, her dusky hair;
But all things else about her drawn
From May-time and the cheerful Dawn;
A dancing Shape, an Image gay,
To haunt, to startle, and way-lay.

I saw her upon nearer view,
A Spirit, yet a Woman too!
Her household motions light and free,
And steps of virgin-liberty;
A countenance in which did meet
Sweet records, promises as sweet;
A Creature not too bright or good
For human nature's daily food;
For transient sorrows, simple wiles,
Praise, blame, love, kisses, tears, and smiles.

And now I see with eye serene
The very pulse of the machine;
A Being breathing thoughtful breath,
A Traveller between life and death;
The reason firm, the temperate will,
Endurance, foresight, strength, and skill;

A perfect Woman, nobly planned,
To warn, to comfort, and command;
And yet a Spirit still, and bright
With something of angelic light.

WILLIAM WORDSWORTH
[1770–1850]

LIFE AND LOVE

*F*ast this Life of mine was dying,
   Blind already and calm as death,
Snowflakes on her bosom lying
   Scarcely heaving with her breath.

Love came by, and having known her
   In a dream of fabled lands,
Gently stooped, and laid upon her
   Mystic chrism of holy hands;

Drew his smile across her folded
   Eyelids, as the swallow dips;
Breathed as finely as the cold did
   Through the locking of her lips.

So, when Life looked upward, being
   Warmed and breathed on from above
What sight could she have for seeing,
   Evermore . . . but only LOVE?

ELIZABETH BARRETT BROWNING
[1806–1861]

MY MISTRESS' EYES

My mistress' eyes are nothing like the sun;
Coral is far more red than her lips' red;
If snow be white, why then her breasts are dun;
If hairs be wires, black wires grow on her head.
I have seen roses damasked, red and white,
But no such roses see I in her cheeks;
And in some perfumes is there more delight
Than in the breath that from my mistress reeks.
I love to hear her speak, yet well I know
That music hath a far more pleasing sound:
I grant I never saw a goddess go;
My mistress, when she walks, treads on the ground.
  And yet, by heaven, I think my love as rare
  As any she belied with false compare.

WILLIAM SHAKESPEARE
[1564–1616]

———

ONE DAY I WROTE HER NAME

One day I wrote her name upon the strand,
But came the waves and washed it away:
Again I wrote it with a second hand,
But came the tide, and made my pains his prey.
"Vain man," said she, "that dost in vain assay,
A mortal thing so to immortalize;
For I myself shall like to this decay,
And eke my name be wiped out likewise."
"Not so," (quod I) "let baser things devise
To die in dust, but you shall live by fame:
My verse your vertues rare shall eternize,
And in the heavens write your glorious name:
Where whenas death shall all the world subdue,
Our love shall live, and later life renew."

EDMUND SPENSER
[1552–1599]

———

"AND FORGIVE US OUR TRESPASSES"

*H*ow prone we are to sin; how sweet were made
The pleasures our resistless hearts invade.
Of all my crimes, the breach of all thy laws,
Love, soft bewitching love, has been the cause.
Of all the paths that vanity has trod,
That sure will soonest be forgiven by God.
If things on earth may be to heaven resembled,
It must be love, pure, constant, undissembled.
But if to sin by chance the charmer press,
Forgive, O Lord, forgive our trespasses.

APHRA BEHN
[1640–1689]

IN THE VALLEY OF CAUTERETZ

All along the valley, stream that flashest white,
Deepening thy voice with the deepening of the night,
All along the valley, where thy waters flow,
I walk'd with one I loved two and thirty years ago.
All along the valley, while I walk'd to-day,
The two and thirty years were a mist that rolls away;
For all along the valley, down thy rocky bed,
Thy living voice to me was as the voice of the dead,
And all along the valley, by rock and cave and tree,
The voice of the dead was a living voice to me.

ALFRED LORD TENNYSON
[1809–1883]

———

BELIEVE ME, IF ALL THOSE
ENDEARING YOUNG CHARMS

Believe me, if all those endearing young charms,
   Which I gaze on so fondly to-day,
Were to change by to-morrow, and fleet in my arms,
   Like fairy-gifts fading away,
Thou wouldst still be adored, as this moment thou art,
   Let thy loveliness fade as it will,
And around the dear ruin each wish of my heart
   Would entwine itself verdantly still.

It is not while beauty and youth are thine own,
   And thy cheeks unprofaned by a tear,
That the fervor and faith of a soul may be known,
   To which time will but make thee more dear!
No, the heart that has truly loved never forgets,
   But as truly loves on to the close,
As the sunflower turns to her god when he sets
   The same look which she turned when he 'rose!

THOMAS MOORE
[1779–1852]

———

THE FIRST DAY

I wish I could remember the first day,
First hour, first moment of your meeting me;
If bright or dim the season, it might be
Summer or winter for aught I can say.
So unrecorded did it slip away,
So blind was I to see and to foresee,
So dull to mark the budding of my tree
That would not blossom yet for many a May.
If only I could recollect it! Such
A day of days! I let it come and go
As traceless as a thaw of bygone snow.
It seemed to mean so little, meant so much!
If only now I could recall that touch,
First touch of hand in hand!—Did one but know!

CHRISTINA ROSSETTI
[1830–1894]

THY LOVE IS BETTER THAN
HIGH BIRTH TO ME

Some glory in their birth, some in their skill,
Some in their wealth, some in their body's force,
Some in their garments, though new-fangled ill,
Some in their hawks and hounds, some in their horse;
And every humor hath his adjunct pleasure,
Wherein it finds a joy above the rest,
But these particulars are not my measure,
All these I better in one general best.
Thy love is [better] than high birth to me,
Richer than wealth, prouder than garments' cost,
Of more delight than hawks or horses be;
And having thee, of all men's pride I boast:
   Wretched in this alone, that thou mayst take
   All this away, and me most wretched make.

WILLIAM SHAKESPEARE
[1564–1616]

107

SONG

She's somewhere in the sunlight strong,
   Her tears are in the falling rain,
She calls me in the wind's soft song,
   And with the flowers she comes again.

Yon bird is but her messenger,
   The moon is but her silver car;
Yea! Sun and moon are sent by her,
   And every wistful, waiting star.

RICHARD LE GALLIENNE
[*dates unknown*]

IF EVER I HAVE THOUGHT OR SAID

If ever I have thought or said
In all the seasons of the past
One word at which thy heart has bled
Believe me, it will be the last.

The tides of life are deep and wide,
The currents swift to bear apart
E'en kindred ships; but from thy side
I pray my sail may never start.

If, in the turning day and night
Of this our earth, our little year,
Thou shalt have lost me from thy sight
Across the checkered spaces drear,

Thy words are uttered; and the mind
Accustomed, cannot all forget;
While written in my heart I find
An impulse that is deeper yet.

We love but never know the things,
To value them, that nearest stand.
The heart that travels seaward brings
The dearest treasure home to land.

PHILIP HENRY SAVAGE
[1868–1899]

MY BEAUTIFUL LADY

I love my lady; she is very fair;
Her brow is white, and bound by simple hair;
    Her spirit sits aloof, and high,
    Altho' it looks thro' her soft eye
    Sweetly and tenderly.

As a young forest, when the wind drives thro',
My life is stirred when she breaks on my view.
    Altho' her beauty has such power,
    Her soul is like the simple flower
    Trembling beneath a shower.

As bliss of saints, when dreaming of large wings,
The bloom around her fancied presence flings,
    I feast and wile her absence, by
    Pressing her choice hand passionately—
    Imagining her sigh.

My lady's voice, altho' so very mild,
Maketh me feel as strong wine would a child;
    My lady's touch, however slight,
    Moves all my senses with its might,
    Like to a sudden fright.

A hawk poised high in air, whose nerved wing-tips
Tremble with might suppressed, before he dips,—
    In vigilance, not more intense

Than I; when her word's gentle sense
Makes full-eyed my suspense.

Her mention of a thing—august or poor,
Makes it seem nobler than it was before:
  As where the sun strikes, life will gush,
  And what is pale receive a flush,
  Rich hues—a richer blush.

THOMAS WOOLNER
[1825–1895]

111

TO ME, FAIR FRIEND,
YOU NEVER CAN BE OLD

To me, fair friend, you never can be old,
For as you were when first your eye I ey'd,
Such seems your beauty still. Three winters cold
Have from the forests shook three summers' pride,
Three beauteous springs to yellow autumn turn'd
In process of the seasons have I seen,
Three April perfumes in three hot Junes burn'd,
Since first I saw you fresh, which yet are green.
Ah, yet doth beauty, like a dial hand,
Steal from his figure, and no pace perceiv'd,
So your sweet hue, which methinks still doth stand,
Hath motion, and mine eye may be deceiv'd;
  For fear of which, hear this, thou age unbred:
  Ere you were born was beauty's summer dead.

WILLIAM SHAKESPEARE
[1564–1616]

THE PRESENCE OF LOVE

And in Life's noisiest hour,
There whispers still the ceaseless Love of Thee,
The heart's *Self-solace* and soliloquy.

You mould my Hopes, you fashion me within;
And to the leading Love-throb in the Heart
Thro' all my Being, thro' my pulses beat;
You lie in all my many Thoughts, like Light,
Like the fair light of Dawn, or summer Eve
On rippling Stream, or cloud-reflecting Lake.
And looking to the Heaven, that bends above you,
How oft! I bless the Lot, that made me love you.

SAMUEL TAYLOR COLERIDGE
[1772–1834]

MOST HAPPY LETTERS

Most happy letters, fram'd by skilful trade,
With which that happy name was first design'd:
That which three times thrice happy hath me made,
With gifts of body, fortune, and of mind.
The first my being to me gave by kind,
From mother's womb deriv'd by due descent,
The second is my sovereign Queen most kind,
That honour and large richesse to me lent.
The third my love, my life's last ornament,
By whom my spirit out of dust was raised:
To speak her praise and glory excellent,
Of all alive most worthy to be praised.
Ye three Elizabeths for ever live,
That three such graces did unto me give.

EDMUND SPENSER
[1552–1599]

———

SERENADE

So sweet the hour, so calm the time,
I feel it more than half a crime,
When Nature sleeps and stars are mute,
To mar the silence ev'n with lute.
At rest on ocean's brilliant dyes
An image of Elysium lies:
Seven Pleiades entranced in Heaven,
Form in the deep another seven:
Endymion nodding from above
Sees in the sea a second love.
Within the valleys dim and brown,
And on the spectral mountain's crown,
The wearied light is dying down,
And earth, and stars, and sea, and sky
Are redolent of sleep, as I
Am redolent of thee and thine
Enthralling love, my Adeline.

EDGAR ALLAN POE
[1809–1849]

———

LOVE IN A LIFE

I

*R*oom after room,
I hunt the house through
We inhabit together.
Heart, fear nothing, for, heart, thou shalt find her—
Next time, herself!—not the trouble behind her
Left in the curtain, the couch's perfume!
As she brushed it, the cornice-wreath blossomed anew:
Yon looking-glass gleamed at the wave of her feather.

II

Yet the day wears,
And door succeeds door;
I try the fresh fortune—
Range the wide house from the wing to the centre.
Still the same chance! she goes out as I enter.
Spend my whole day in the quest,—who cares?
But 'tis twilight, you see,—with such suites to explore,
Such closets to search, such alcoves to importune!

ROBERT BROWNING
[1812–1889]

MY LOVE IN HER ATTIRE

My love in her attire doth show her wit,
    It doth so well become her:
For every season she hath dressings fit,
    For winter, spring, and summer.
    No beauty she doth miss,
    When all her robes are on:
    But Beauty's self she is,
    When all her robes are gone.

ANONYMOUS

THE INDIAN SERENADE

I arise from dreams of thee
In the first sweet sleep of night,
When the winds are breathing low,
And the stars are shining bright
I arise from dreams of thee,
And a spirit in my feet
Hath led me—who knows how?
To thy chamber window, Sweet!

The wandering airs they faint
On the dark, the silent stream—
The champak odors fail
Like sweet thoughts in a dream;
The nightingale's complaint,
It dies upon her heart;
As I must on thine,
Oh, beloved as thou art!

O lift me from the grass!
I die! I faint! I fail!
Let thy love in kisses rain
On my lips and eyelids pale.
My cheek is cold and white, alas!
My heart beats loud and fast;—
Oh! press it to thine own again,
Where it will break at last.

PERCY BYSSHE SHELLEY
[1792–1822]

TO ASRA

Are there two things, of all which men possess,
That are so like each other and so near,
As mutual Love seems like to Happiness?
Dear Asra, woman beyond utterance dear!
This Love which ever welling at my heart,
Now in its living fount doth heave and fall,
Now overflowing pours thro' every part
Of all my frame, and fills and changes all,
Like vernal waters springing up through snow,
This Love that seeming great beyond the power
Of growth, yet seemeth ever more to grow,
Could I transmute the whole to one rich Dower
Of Happy Life, and give it all to Thee,
Thy lot, methinks, were Heaven, thy age, Eternity!

SAMUEL TAYLOR COLERIDGE
[1772–1834]

THE REVELATION

An idle poet, here and there,
Looks around him; but, for all the rest,
The world, unfathomably fair,
Is duller than a witling's jest.
Love wakes men, once a lifetime each;
They lift their heavy lids, and look;
And, lo, what one sweet page can teach,
They read with joy, then shut the book.
And some give thanks, and some blaspheme
And most forget; but, either way,
That and the Child's unheeded dream
Is all the light of all their day.

COVENTRY PATMORE
[1823–1896]

OH! THAT WE TWO WERE MAYING

❁

Oh! that we two were Maying
Down the stream of the soft spring breeze;
Like children with violets playing
In the shade of the whispering trees.

Oh! that we two sat dreaming
On the sward of some sheep-trimmed down,
Watching the white mist steaming
Over river and mead and town.

Oh! that we two lay sleeping
In our nest in the churchyard sod,
With our limbs at rest on the quiet earth's breast,
And our souls at home with God!

CHARLES KINGSLEY
[1819–1875]

A RED, RED ROSE

O, my luve is like a red, red rose,
   That's newly sprung in June.
O my luve is like the melodie
   That's sweetly played in tune.

As fair art thou, my bonnie lass,
   So deep in luve am I,
And I will luve thee still, my dear,
   Till a' the seas gang dry.

Till a' the seas gang dry, my dear,
   And the rocks melt wi' the sun!
And I will luve thee still, my dear,
   While the sands o' life shall run.

And fare thee weel, my only luve,
   And fare thee weel awhile!
And I will come again, my luve,
   Though it were ten thousand mile!

ROBERT BURNS
[1759–1796]

_____

TO MY DEAR AND LOVING HUSBAND

If ever two were one then surely we.
If ever man were loved by wife, then thee;
If ever wife were happy in a man,
Compare with me, ye women, if you can.
I prize thy love more than whole mines of gold
Or all the riches that the East doth hold.
My love is such that rivers cannot quench,
Nor aught but love from thee give recompense.
Thy love is such I can no way repay,
The heavens reward thee manifold, I pray.
Then while we live, in love let's so perservere
That when we live no more, we may live ever.

ANNE BRADSTREET
[1612–1672]

INDEX

OF AUTHORS

Anonymous
  My Love in Her Attire, 117
Apache (Traditional)
  Wedding Prayer, 58
Aldrich, Thomas Bailey
  Love's Calendar, 90
Beddoes, Thomas Lovell
  Song, 95
Behn, Aphra
  *"And Forgive Us Our
    Trespasses,"* 103
  Dream, The, 7
Best, Charles
  Sonnet of the Moon, A, 16
Betham-Edwards, Mathilda
  Valentine, A, 17
Bible, The
  Song of Songs, The (from
    Chapter 2), 5
Bradstreet, Anne
  *To My Dear and Loving Hus-
    band,* 123
Brainard, John
  String Around My Finger, The,
    38-39
  To ——— , 9
Browning, Elizabeth Barrett

  How Do I Love Thee?, 85
  I Lived With Visions, 37
  If Thou Must Love Me, 78
  Life and Love, 100
  Love I Bear Thee, The, 50
Browning, Robert
  Love in a Life, 116
  Meeting at Night, 44
  My Star, 48
Bulwer-Lytton, see Lytton
Burns, Robert
  Red, Red Rose, A, 122
Byron, Lord
  She Walks in Beauty, 47
Campbell, (Major Robert)
  Calder
  Sonnet, 6
Carew, Thomas
  *Song: When June is Past, the
    Fading Rose, A,* 36
Clare, John
  I Hid My Love, 18
  Summer, 22

Coleridge, Samuel Taylor
  Desire, 49
  Presence of Love, The, 113

To Asra, 119
Cook, Eliza
  Don't Tell the World That You're
    Waiting for Me, 69
Daniel, Samuel
  Delia (34), 97
Donne, John
  Air and Angels, 27-28
Dyer, Sir Edward
  Love is Love, 92
Emerson, Ralph Waldo
  Give All to Love, 41-42
Feltham, Owen
  When, Dearest, I But Think on
    Thee, 83-84
Ford, Thomas
  Thomas Ford's Music of Sundry
    Kinds (excerpt), 11-12
Graham, James, Marquis of
    Montrose
  My Dear and Only Love, 70-71
Greenwood, Grace
  Love's Emblems, 94
  Valentines (written for Miss
    L——'s Valentine Parties), 24
Herbert, George
  Love, 33
Herrick, Robert
  To Anthea, Who May Com-
    mand Him Anything, 67-68
Hovey, Richard
  Thought of Her, The, 20
Howard, Henry, Earl of Surrey
  Praise of His Love, A, 72-73
Hunt, Leigh
  Jenny Kissed Me, 35
Johnson, James Weldon
  Beauty That is Never Old, 61
Jonson, Ben
  Come, My Celia, 63
  To Celia, 60

Kingsley, Charles
  Oh! That We Two Were Maying,
    121
Le Gallienne, Richard
  Song, 108
Lovelace, Richard
  Song to Amarantha, That She
    Would Dishevel Her Hair,
    45-46
Lytton, Edward Bulwer-Lytton,
    Baron
  Absent Yet Present, 31-32
Marlowe, Christopher
  Passionate Shepherd to His
    Love, The, 74-75
Marvell, Andrew
  Definition of Love, The, 29-30
  Fair Singer, The, 25
Moore, Thomas
  Believe Me, If All Those En-
    dearing Young Charms, 105
Morley, Thomas
  On a Fair Morning, As I Came
    by the Way, 53
Morris, William
  Love is Enough: Song I, 79
O'Reilly, John Boyle
  White Rose, A, 10
Patmore, Coventry
  Revelation, The, 120
Poe, Edgar Allan
  Dream Within a Dream, A, 13
  Serenade, 115
  Song, 62
  To F—— , 96
Raleigh, Sir Walter
  Nymph's Reply to the Shep-
    herd, The, 76-77
Rossetti, Christina
  Birthday, A, 34
  First Day, The, 106

Rossetti, Dante Gabriel
    Sudden Light, 26
Savage, Philip Henry
    If Ever I Have Thought or Said,
      109
    To Citriodora, 8
Sedley, Sir Charles
    To Celia, 57
Shakespeare, William
    Marriage of True Minds, The, 93
    My Mistress' Eyes, 101
    Shall I Compare Thee, 65
    Those Lips That Love's Own
      Hand Did Make, 19
    Thy Love is Better Than High
      Birth to Me, 107
    To Me, Fair Friend, You Can
      Never Be Old, 112
Shelley, Percy Bysshe
    Indian Serenade, The, 118
    Love's Philosophy, 3
    Music, When Soft Voices Die, 89
    To Jane, 80–81
Sherman, Frank Dempster
    Love's Springtide, 21
Sill, Edward Rowland
    Open Window, The, 14–15
Spencer, Edmund
    Most Happy Letters, 114

    One Day I Wrote Her Name,
      102
Stevenson, Robert Louis
    I Will Make You Brooches, 59
Teasdale, Sara
    After Parting, 82
    Kiss, The, 52
    Look, The, 23
    Years, The, 4
Tennyson, Alfred Lord
    In the Valley of Cauteretz, 104
Thomson, James
    Art (excerpt), 91
    Sunday up the River (excerpt),
      51
    Wine of Love, The, 54
Waller, Edmund
    On a Girdle, 40
Wilbye, John
    Love Me Not for Comely
      Grace, 43
Wilcox, Ella Wheeler
    Love Thyself Last, 66
Woolner, Thomas
    My Beautiful Lady, 110–111
Wordsworth, William
    Most Sweet It Is, 64
    She Was a Phantom of Delight,
      98–99

INDEX OF FIRST LINES

All along the valley, stream that flashest white	104
All that I know	48
All trembling in my arms Aminta lay	7
Amarantha sweet and fair	45–46
An idle poet, here and there	120
And in Life's noisiest hour	113
And wilt thou have me fashion into speech	50
Are there two things, of all which men possess	119
As the flight of a river	31–32
Ask me no more where Jove bestows	36
Before you kissed me only winds of heaven	52
Believe me, if all those endearing young charms	105
Beloved! amid the earnest woes	96
Bid me to live, and I will live	67–68
Come live with me and be my love	74–75
Come, my celia, let us prove	63
Come we to the summer, to the summer we will come	22
Drink to me only with thine eyes	60
Fast this Life of mine was dying	100
Give a man a horse he can ride	51
Give all to love;	41–42
Give place, ye lovers, here before	72–73
How do I love thee? Let me count the ways.	85
How many times do I love thee, dear?	95
How prone we are to sin; how sweet were made	103
I arise from dreams of thee	118

I have been here before   26
I hid my love when young till I   18
I lived with visions for my company   37
I love my lady; she is very fair;   110-111
I saw thee on thy bridal day —   62
I turn and see you passing in the street   8
I will make you brooches and toys for your delight   59
I wish I could remember the first day   106
If all the world and love were young   76-77
If ever I have thought or said   109
If ever two were one then surely we   123
If thou must love me, let it be for nought   78
Jenny kissed me when we met   35
Let me not to the marriage of true minds   93
Look how the pale queen of the silent night   16
Love bade me welcome; yet my soul drew back   33
Love is enough: though the World be a-waning   79
Love me not for comely grace   43
Love thyself last. Look near, behold thy duty   66
Most happy letters, fram'd by skilful trade   114
Most sweet it is with unuplifted eyes   64
Music, when soft voices die   89
My dear and only Love, I pray   70-71
My heart is like a singing bird   34
My heart was winter-bound until   21
My love for thee doth take me unaware   20
My love in her attire doth show her wit   117
My love is of a birth as rare   29-30
My mistress' eyes are nothing like the sun;   101
My tower was grimly builded   14-15
Not, Celia, that I juster am   57
Now you will feel no rain   58
O, my luve is like a red, red rose   122
Oh I have sown my love so wide   82
Oh! that we two were Maying   121
On a fair morning, as I came by the way   53
One day I wrote her name upon the strand   102
Room after room   116
Shall I compare thee to a summer's day?   65
She walks in beauty, like the night   47
— She was a lovely one — her shape was light   9

She was a Phantom of delight   98–99
She's somewhere in the sunlight strong   108
So sweet the hour, so calm the time   115
Some glory in their birth, some in their skill   107
Strephon kissed me in the spring   23
Take this kiss upon the brow!   13
That which her slender waist confin'd   40
The bell that strikes the warning hour   38–39
The fountains mingle with the river   3
The grey sea and the long black land;   44
The keen stars were twinkling   80–81
The lowest trees have tops, the ant her gall   92
The red rose whispers of passion   10
The Summer comes and the Summer goes;   90
The voice of my beloved!   5
The wine of Love is music   54
There is a lady sweet and kind   11–12
There was a rose, that blushing grew   94
Those lips that Love's own hand did make   19
Three summers have gone since the first time we met, love   69
To make a final conquest of all me   25
To me, fair friend, you can never be old   112
To-night I close my eyes and see   4
Twice or thrice had I lov'd thee   27–28
We never met; yet to my soul   24
What precious thing are you making fast   91
What shall I send my sweet today   17
When buffeted and beaten by life's storms   61
When, dearest, I but think on thee   83–84
When midst the summer-roses the warm bees   6
When winter snows upon thy golden hairs   97
Where true Love burns Desire is Love's pure flame;   49

ABOUT THE AUTHOR

With a degree in English literature, KATHLEEN BLEASE first served as an editor for two major publishing houses before starting out on her own as a freelance book editor and writer. Over the span of her career, she has written on a variety of topics—from health to education to home improvements to parenthood—and edited books that have won acclaim throughout the country.

Four years ago, her love unexpectedly knocked on her front door and introduced himself, and Kathleen's vision of life changed forever. Today, she finds that the blessings and lessons of family and love are the most intriguing topics of all, and she writes about their powers and comforts.

Kathleen's other poetry collections are *A Friend Is Forever: Precious Poems That Celebrate the Beauty of Friendship* and *A Mother's Love: Classic Poems Celebrating the Maternal Heart.*

She lives with her husband, Roger, and their two children in the historic district of Easton, Pennsylvania.